# Inner Peace

CLASSIC WISDOM COLLECTION

# Inner Peace

## Wisdom from Jean-Pierre de Caussade

Edited and with a foreword by Kathryn Hermes, FSP

*auline*
BOOKS & MEDIA
Boston

Library of Congress Cataloging-in-Publication Data

Caussade, Jean Pierre de, d. 1751.

 [Abandon à la providence divine. English. Selections]

 Inner peace : wisdom from Jean-Pierre de Caussade / edited and with a foreword by Kathryn Hermes.

  p. cm. -- (Classic wisdom collection)

 Translation of selections from the author's Abandon à la providence divine, and correspondence.

 ISBN 0-8198-3705-9 (pbk.)

 1. Mysticism--Catholic Church. 2. Spiritual life--Catholic Church. 3. Caussade, Jean Pierre de, d. 1751.--Correspondence. I. Hermes, Kathryn. II. Caussade, Jean Pierre de, d. 1751. Correspondence. English. Selections. III. Title. IV. Series.

 BV5082.3.C3813 2011

 248.2'2--dc22

                            2010038173

Unless otherwise noted: The Scripture quotations contained herein are from the *New Revised Standard Version Bible: Catholic Edition*, copyright © 1989, 1993, Division of Christian Education of the National Council of the Churches of Christ in the United States of America. Used by permission. All rights reserved.

Excerpts from the 1921 B. Herder Book Company publication of *Abandonment to Divine Providence* have been edited to reflect current English style and usage.

Cover design by Rosana Usselmann

Cover photo by Mary Louise Winters, FSP

Published by Pauline Books & Media, 50 Saint Pauls Avenue, Boston, MA 02130-3491

Printed in the U.S.A.

www.pauline.org

Pauline Books & Media is the publishing house of the Daughters of St. Paul, an international congregation of women religious serving the Church with the communications media.

2 3 4 5 6 7 8 9                                     17 16 15 14 13

*With gratitude to*
*Harold and Adelaide Steffes*
*and Mary and Jack Schuler*
*for teaching me*
*the beauty of a life*
*lived in peace*

# Contents

XXII

Peace and Confidence

Notes

# Foreword

Jean-Pierre de Caussade found me when I was 23. Twenty-four months before, I had been visited by a stroke. In the space of a day, my early adult years, so full of promise, were filled with dark and confusing cloud formations that cast their long shadows across my mind and heart. One day I could do whatever I set my mind to, the next I needed help with everything. One day I could express myself clearly with a broad vocabulary, the next I could only mumble and couldn't recall even the most basic words. One day I was in charge, the next . . . I guess that was the main question: Was anyone in charge? Did anyone really know what was happening to me? Did anyone care? Was this all a punishment? Would I recover? What would the rest of my life be like?

Questions, worries, and fears swept away the balmy days following my religious profession a year before. In the middle of the storm that raged in my thoughts and desires came the voice of calm and promise, the voice of Jean-Pierre de Caussade. Next to me, as I write these words is my first copy of his book *Abandonment to Divine Providence*.[1] It still looks almost brand new, so carefully have I preserved this book, which became a lifeline for me. Only the frayed edges along the backbone and the $3.50 price marked on the top right-hand corner betray its almost thirty years of age. Those were the days of simple covers, so nothing spectacular would have drawn me to pick up the book. I can explain the attraction only as Caussade seeking me out and God reaching down to me in my confusion and tears.

I remember those first months after my discovery. How I treasured this book. The sentence at the end of the first section was for me like the first rays of sun streaming through the thunder clouds after an angry storm: "[Mary's] spirit, transported with joy, looked upon all that she had to do or to suffer at each moment as the gift of him who fills with good things the hearts of those who hunger and thirst for him alone, and have no desire for created things."[2] *Transported with joy . . . gifts . . . good things. . . .* Every morning before I went to chapel I stopped and read another paragraph, and for the past twenty odd years I haven't stopped sitting before this man, who has become my mentor.

The stroke was neither the first nor the last "gift" I have received in my life that I have found difficult to call "good." There have been others, as there are in every adult life. When my mind is swirling with plans, worries, analyses, discouragement—in a word, non-peace—I always look on my bookshelf for this little book by Caussade. It has also led others with whom I have shared his teaching to great peace of mind.

I must confess that problems and pains still catch me off guard; world and ecclesial situations disappoint and disillusion me, and I become stressed and exhausted. At these times, I lose my peace of mind. However, I know where to go to restore my inner peace. I pick up my copy of *Abandonment* and touch once again the abyss of peace and contentment with God, whose divine action I can see revealed everywhere in me and around me.

───── ❧ ─────

Who was Jean-Pierre de Caussade? He was born in 1675 and died in 1751. We know he entered the Jesuit novitiate in 1693. We know from that point on where he was assigned as a Jesuit, but his personal story remains shrouded in history. There were many great spiritual writers of that period. He was not one of them. However, his writings gained popularity in the twentieth century. In fact, he never knew he wrote the book *Abandonment to Divine Providence*.

In 1729, Caussade arrived in Nancy, in the Lorraine province of France, and became director of the Visitation nuns. He remained there just a year, and then returned there in 1733 for a nearly six-year stay before being transferred again. The superiors of the Visitation monastery carefully preserved the letters and conferences that he gave the nuns at Nancy. In the 1800s, they gave these letters to a learned French Jesuit, Father Henri Ramière, who, in 1861, edited them and published a small volume. The book at once found many readers, and with each new edition Ramière incorporated new material. It has been translated into many languages and published in many editions under different names.

Caussade's spiritual doctrine is so simple, and so clear is his vision of God's activity in his life, you can summarize it in only a few words: *trustful surrender in every duty and event, for in them God is secretly at work for your good.* To every doubt, trouble, desolation, and trial the nuns at Nancy shared with him, he applied this same solution but with perfect tact to the needs and state of each of them. What a treasure is ours to leaf through the letters and read the practical yet profound way he leads each person to inner peace and complete trust in God. Step by step, he guides each person to the most heroic abandonment and intimate union with God. In the letters, he also tells us about himself. When he left the quiet life as spiritual director at the Visitation monastery, his superiors reassigned him to an administrative role in which he had to deal with business he knew nothing about—finances, negotiations, conflict resolution. Although he loved silence and solitude, he found that God came to his aid and helped him to find peace in the midst of all he had been asked to do.

Though Caussade held many important posts in the Society of Jesus, his letters reveal that he was a simple man. What mattered most to him were the necessity of loving God and surrendering to him completely, moment by moment. We need not fret over the past nor worry about the future. We are given only the sacrament of the present moment in which God reveals himself to us in the midst of our daily duty and daily events. We need not do anything extraordinary. All we must do is our Christian duty. Attention to even the smallest of trivialities as a sacrament of God's revelation will bring us complete inner peace and lead us as close to God as is possible.

The selections in this book are from the volume edited by Father Henri Ramière, the theoretical presentation of Caussade's teaching, and the original letters he wrote. The letters, which are his sensitive and practical application of this teaching to individuals, reveal the way he himself lived this doctrine.

———— ❧ ————

*Abandonment to Divine Providence* found me again in my middle adult years. Like other adults, responsibility, deadlines, and expectations stretch and stress me. I have had my share of heartaches, reversals, disillusionments, bitter blows, and failure. A couple of years ago, I became terribly disillusioned over a situation. As I struggled for months regarding a decision, I stumbled again upon the key teaching of *Abandonment*. I didn't read it in the pages of the book. I unearthed it from deep within my own heart, which has been shaped by Caussade's teaching for almost thirty years. "God," I prayed, "if you do not wish this project to go ahead, then let me know. I will no longer carry it forward. I sincerely believed that this is what you wanted. But if that is not so, then I am willing to set it aside without another word." I immediately felt such profound peace of soul. My angry thoughts were stilled. My fears of failure and humiliation were quieted. The burden was lifted, and I was freed.

Stress comes from this wrestling match, often unconscious, between what we are pursuing and what simply is unfolding from the heart of God. Once we bring these elements into realignment, our minds find peace.

As you embark on this wonderful journey of faith with such an able guide as Father de Caussade, keep in mind a few simple principles:

- ❖ Abandonment is the center of a solid peace.
- ❖ Leave all to God, and all will go well.
- ❖ Do not imagine problems where they don't exist.
- ❖ Want things to be exactly as they are.
- ❖ Do everything in your power, and leave the rest to God.
- ❖ God will direct you moment by moment through the ordinary events of your daily life. Be prepared to be surprised!

The secret of abandonment to Divine Providence is not that you must give up your own will to do what God wants. Instead, it is the wondrous discovery that we have the unspeakable privilege of being instruments in the hands of God, that God treats us with such dignity as his partners in creation. Our life has meaning as we work out God's hallowed designs, and, in doing so, we find that all our deepest desires are met. As the years pass we marvel at the synchronicity of events—both pleasant and difficult situations—that blend together in a might symphony of joy. Ultimately, we find great peace of mind and soul because we have nothing to achieve or defend. We can carry out our daily duties quietly, without anxiety, without hurry, without uneasiness about the future because we have touched with our own hands the fatherly providence of God for us and learned that relying upon that providence is the best way to secure our lives both now and in the future.

# I

# Sanctity Found in Fidelity

God continues to speak today as he spoke in former times to our fathers when there were no directors as we have presently, nor any regular method of direction. At that time all spirituality was comprised in fidelity to the designs of God, for there was no detail, nor so many instructions, precepts, and examples as there are now. Doubtless our present difficulties render this direction necessary and straightforward. In earlier times, those who led a spiritual life found that each moment brought some duty to be faithfully accomplished. Their whole attention was thus directed like the hand of a clock that marks the hours. Their minds, incessantly animated by the inflowing of divine grace, turned imperceptibly to each new duty that presented itself by the permission of God at different hours of the day.

Such were the hidden springs from which sprung the conduct of Mary. Mary was the most simple of all creatures and the most closely united to God. Her answer to the angel when she said, "May it be done unto me according to your will"—*"Fiat mihi secundum verbum tuum"* (cf. Lk 1:38)—contained all the mystic theology of her ancestors reduced to the purest, simplest submission of the soul to the will of God, under whatever form it presented itself. This beautiful and exalted state, which was the basis of the spiritual life of Mary, shines conspicuously in these simple words, *"Fiat mihi."* Take notice that they are in complete harmony with those which our Lord desires that we should have always on our lips and in our hearts: "Your will be done"—*"Fiat voluntas tua"* (Mt 6:10).

It is true that what was required of Mary at this great moment would result in her very great glory, but the magnificence of this glory would have made no impression on her if she had not seen the fulfillment of the will of God in it. In all things was she ruled by the divine will. Whether her occupations were ordinary, or of an elevated nature, they were to her the manifestation, at times obscure, at times clear, of the operations of the Most High. In all things she saw the glory of God. Her spirit, transported with joy, looked upon all that she had to do or to suffer at each moment as the gift of him who fills with good things the hearts of those who hunger and thirst for him alone and have no desire for created things.

— Excerpt from *Abandonment to Divine Providence*,
Book 1: Chapter 1, Section 1.

## II

# A Hidden Treasure

"The power of the Most High will overshadow you" (Lk 1:35), said the angel to Mary. This shadow under which the power of God hides for the purpose of bringing forth Jesus Christ in the soul, is the duty, the attraction, or the cross that is presented to us at each moment. These are, in reality, merely shadows like those in the order of nature which cover sensible objects like a veil and thus hide them from us. Therefore, in the moral and supernatural order, the duties of each moment conceal, under the semblance of dark shadows, the truth of their divine character on which alone we should fix our attention. It was in this light that Mary beheld them. Also these shadows diffused over her faculties, far from creating illusion, served only to increase her faith in him who is unchanging and unchangeable. The archangel may depart. He has delivered his message, and his moment has passed. Mary, instead, advances without ceasing and is already far beyond him. The Holy Spirit, who comes to take possession of her under the shadow of the angel's word, will never abandon her.

There are remarkably few extraordinary characteristics in the outward events of the life of the most holy Virgin, at least there are none recorded in Holy Scripture. Her exterior life is represented as very ordinary and simple. She did and suffered the same things that anyone in a similar state of life might do or suffer. She goes to visit her cousin Elizabeth as her other relatives did. She took shelter in a stable because she was poor. She returned to Nazareth out of which she had been driven by the persecution of Herod and lived there with Jesus and Joseph. They supported themselves by the work of their hands. It was in this way that the holy family gained their daily bread. But what a divine nourishment Mary and Joseph received from this daily bread for the strengthening of their faith! It is like a sacrament to sanctify all their moments. What treasures of grace lie concealed in these moments filled, apparently, by the most ordinary events. That which is visible might have happened to anyone, but the invisible discerned by faith is nothing less than God bringing about very great things. O Bread of Angels! Heavenly Manna! Pearl of the Gospel! Sacrament of the present moment! You give God under as lowly a form as the manger, the hay, or the straw. And to whom do you give him? *"Esurientes implevit bonis"*— "He has filled the hungry with good things . . ." (Lk 1:53). God reveals himself to the humble under the most lowly of forms, but the proud, who fix their gaze entirely on that which is extrinsic, never discover him hidden beneath, and are sent away empty.

— Excerpt from *Abandonment to Divine Providence*,
Book 1: Chapter 1, Section 2.

## III

# Uncomplicated Sanctity

If the work of our sanctification seems to present insurmountable difficulties, it is because we do not know how to form a true idea of it. In reality, sanctity can be reduced to one single practice: fidelity to one's duties as appointed by God. Now this fidelity is equally within each person's power, either in its active practice or in its passive exercise.

The active practice of fidelity consists in accomplishing the duties imposed on us by the general laws of God and of the Church or by the particular state in life we may have embraced. Its passive exercise, on the other hand, consists in the loving acceptance of all that God sends us at each moment.

Are either of these practices of sanctity above our strength? Certainly not the active fidelity, since the duties it imposes cease to be duties when we have no longer the power to fulfill them. If the state of your health does not permit you to go to Mass, you are not obliged to go. The same rule holds good for all the precepts laid down by the Church; that is to say, for all those which prescribe specific duties. Only those rules which forbid evil in themselves are absolute, since it is never permissible to commit sin. Could there be anything more reasonable?

What excuse can be made? Yet this is all that God requires of the soul for the work of its sanctification. He exacts it from both high and low, from the strong and the weak, in a word from all, always, and everywhere. It is true, therefore, that he requires on our part only simple and easy things since it is only necessary to employ this single method to attain to an eminent degree of sanctity. If, over and above the commandments, God shows us the counsels as a more perfect aim, he always takes care to suit the practice of them to our position and character. He bestows on us, as the principal sign of our vocation to follow them, the attractions of grace which make them easy. He never impels anyone beyond his strength nor in any manner beyond his aptitude. Again, what could be more just? All you who strive after perfection and who are tempted to discouragement at the remembrance of what you have read in the lives of the saints and of what certain pious books prescribe; O you who are appalled by the terrible ideals of perfection you have formed for yourselves; it is for your consolation that God has willed me to write this. Learn that of which you seem to be ignorant. This God of all goodness has made those things easy which are common and necessary in the order of nature, such as breathing, eating, and sleeping. No less necessary in the supernatural order are love and fidelity, therefore, it cannot be that means of acquiring them is as difficult as it is generally made out to be. Review your life. Is it not composed of innumerable actions of very little importance? Well, God is quite satisfied with these. They are the share that the soul must take in the work of its perfection. This is so clearly explained in Holy Scripture that there can be no doubt about it: "Fear God, and keep his commandments; for that is the whole duty of everyone" (Eccl 12:13), that is to say—this is all that is required and it is in this that active fidelity consists. If we fulfill our part, God will do the rest. Grace is bestowed only on this condition, and the marvels it effects are beyond our comprehension. For neither ear has heard nor eye seen, nor has it entered the mind what things God has planned in his omniscience, determined in his will, and carried out by his power in the souls given up entirely to him.

The passive part of sanctity is even easier since it consists simply in accepting that which we very often have no power to prevent and in suffering lovingly, that is to say with sweetness and consolation, those things that so often cause weariness and disgust. Once more I repeat, sanctity consists in this. This is the grain of mustard seed which is the smallest of all the seeds, the fruits of which can neither be recognized nor gathered. It is the drachma of the Gospel, the treasure that none discover because they suppose it to be too far away to be sought. Do not ask me how this treasure can be found. It is no secret. The treasure is everywhere, it is offered to us at all times and wherever we may be. All creatures, both friends and enemies pour it out with prodigality and it flows like a fountain through every faculty of body and soul even to the very center of our hearts. If we open our mouths they will be filled. The divine activity permeates the whole universe, it pervades every creature. Wherever they are it is there. It goes before them, with them, and it follows them. All they have to do is to let the waves bear them on.

Would to God that kings and their ministers, princes of the Church and of the world, priests and soldiers, the peasantry and laborers, in a word, all could know how very easy it would be for them to arrive at a high degree of sanctity. They would only have to fulfill the simple duties of Christianity and of their state of life; to embrace with submission the crosses belonging to that state and to submit with faith and love to the designs of Providence in all those things that have to be done or suffered, without going out of their way to seek occasions for themselves. This is the spirit by which the patriarchs and prophets were animated and sanctified before there were so many systems from so many masters of the spiritual life. This is the spirituality of all ages and of every state. No state of life can, assuredly, be sanctified in a more exalted manner, nor in a more wonderful and easy way than by the simple use of the means that God, the sovereign Director of souls, gives them at each moment to do or to suffer.

— Excerpt from *Abandonment to Divine Providence*,
Book 1: Chapter 1, Section 3.

# IV

# God's Action

All creatures that exist are in the hands of God. The action of the creature can only be perceived by the senses, but faith sees in all things the action of the Creator. It believes that in Jesus Christ all things live and that his divine operation continues to the end of time, embracing the passing moment and the smallest created atom in its hidden life and mysterious action. The work of the creature is a veil which covers the profound mysteries of the divine operation. After the resurrection Jesus Christ took his disciples by surprise in his various appearances. He showed himself to them under various disguises and, in the act of making himself known to them, disappeared.

This same Jesus, ever living, ever working, still takes by surprise those souls whose faith is weak and wavering.

There is not a moment in which God does not present himself under the disguise of some pain to be endured, of some consolation to be enjoyed, or of some duty to be performed. All which takes place within us, around us, or through us, contains and conceals God's divine action.

His action is really and truly present, but invisibly so, in such a way that we are always surprised and don't recognize his activity until it has ceased. If we could lift the veil and if we were attentive and watchful, God would continually reveal himself to us, and we should see his divine action in everything that happened to us and rejoice in it. At each successive occurrence we would exclaim: "It is the Lord!" and we would accept every fresh circumstance as God's gift. We would look upon creatures as feeble tools in the hands of an able workman and realize that nothing was wanting to us, that the constant providence of God disposed him to bestow upon us at every moment whatever we required. If only we had faith we should show goodwill to all creatures. We should cherish them and be interiorly grateful to them as serving, by God's will, our salvation. If we lived the life of faith without intermission we would have an uninterrupted union with God and a constant familiar conversation with him. What the air is for the transmission of our thoughts and words, our actions and sufferings would be for those of God. They would be as the substance of his word and in all external events we would see nothing but what was excellent and holy.

This union is effected on earth by faith, in heaven by glory; the only difference is in the method of its working. God is interpreted by faith. Without the light of faith creation would speak to us in vain. It is a writing in cipher which would yield nothing but confusion and chaos out of which no one would expect to hear the voice of God. But as Moses saw the fire of divine charity in the burning bush, so faith gives us the clue to the cipher and reveals to us, in this mass of confusion, marvels of divine wisdom.

Faith changes the face of the earth. By it the heart is raised, entranced, and becomes conversant with heavenly things. Faith is our light in this life. By it we possess the truth without seeing it; we touch what we cannot feel and see what is not evident to the senses. By it we view the world as though it didn't exist. Faith is the key of the treasure house, the key of the abyss of the science of God. It is faith that teaches us the hollowness of created things. By although continually warned that everything that happens in the world is but a shadow, a figure, a mystery of faith, we look at exterior events only and do not perceive the enigma they contain?

We fall into this trap like senseless people, instead of raising our eyes to the principle, source, and origin of all things in which they all have their right name and just proportions, in which everything is supernatural, divine, and sanctifying, in which all is part of the plenitude of Jesus Christ and each circumstance a stone toward the construction of the heavenly Jerusalem, and in which all helps to build a dwelling for us in that marvelous city.

We live according to what we see and feel, and as a consequence wander like madmen in a labyrinth of darkness and illusion for want of the light of faith which would guide us safely through it. By means of faith we would be able to aspire after God and to live for him alone, forsaking and going beyond mere figures.

— Excerpt from *Abandonment to Divine Providence*,
Book 1: Chapter 2, Section 1.

# V

# Enlightened by Faith

The soul enlightened by faith judges things in a very different way than those who, having only the standard of the senses by which to measure them, ignore the inestimable treasure they contain. The one who knows that a certain person in disguise is the king, behaves toward him very differently than another who, only perceiving him to be an ordinary man, treats him accordingly. In the same way, the soul that recognizes the will of God in the smallest event as well as in those that are the most distressing, receives all things with an equal joy, pleasure, and respect. Such a soul throws open its doors to receive with honor what others fear and flee from with horror. The outward appearance may be mean and contemptible, but beneath this abject garb the heart discovers and honors the majesty of the King. The deeper the abasement of his entry in such a guise and the more secret, the greater does the heart become filled with love. I cannot describe what the heart feels when it accepts the divine will in such humble, poor and lowly disguises. Ah! How the sight of God, poor and humble, lodged in a stable, lying on straw, weeping and trembling, pierced the loving heart of Mary! Ask the inhabitants of Bethlehem what they thought of the child. You know what answer they gave, and how they would have paid court to him had he been lodged in a palace surrounded by the state due to princes.

Then ask Mary and Joseph, the magi, and the shepherds. They will tell you that they found in this extreme poverty an indescribable tenderness and an infinite dignity worthy of the majesty of God. Faith is strengthened, increased, and enriched by those things that escape the senses. The less there is to see, the more there is to believe. To adore Jesus on Tabor, to accept the will of God in extraordinary circumstances does not indicate a life animated by great faith as much as loving the will of God in ordinary things and adoring Jesus on the cross. For faith cannot be said to be a real, living faith until it is tried and has triumphed over every effort for its destruction. War with the senses enables faith to obtain a more glorious victory. To consider God equally good in things that are petty and ordinary as in those which are great and uncommon is to have a faith that is not common, but great and extraordinary.

. . . Mary, when the apostles fled, remained steadfast at the foot of the cross. She owned Jesus as her son when he was disfigured with wounds and covered with mud and spittle. The wounds that disfigured him made him only more lovable and adorable in the eyes of this tender mother. The more awful were the blasphemies uttered against him, so much the deeper became her veneration and respect.

The life of faith is nothing less than the continued pursuit of God through all that disguises, disfigures, destroys, and, as it were, destroys him. It is in very truth a reproduction of the life of Mary who, from the stable to the cross, remained unalterably united to that God who all the world misunderstood, abandoned, and persecuted. In like manner faithful souls endure a constant succession of trials. God hides beneath veils of darkness and illusive appearances which make his will difficult to recognize; but in spite of every obstacle these souls follow him and love him even to death on the cross. They know that, leaving the darkness they must run after the light of this divine sun which, from its rising to its setting, however dark and thick may be the clouds that obscure it, enlightens, warms, and inflames the faithful hearts that bless, praise, and contemplate it during the whole circle of its mysterious course.

Pursue then without ceasing, you faithful souls, this beloved Spouse who with giant strides passes from one end of the heavens to the other. If you be content and untiring, nothing will have power to hide him from you. He moves above the smallest blades of grass as above the mighty cedar. The grains of sand are under his feet as well as the huge mountain. Wherever you may turn, there you will find his footprints, and in following them perseveringly you will find him wherever you may be.

Oh! What delightful peace we enjoy when we have learned by faith to find God thus in all his creatures! Then is darkness luminous and bitterness sweet. Faith, while showing us things as they are, changes their ugliness into beauty and their malice into virtue. Faith is the mother of sweetness, confidence, and joy. It cannot help feeling tenderness and compassion for its enemies by whose means it is so immeasurably enriched. The greater the harshness and severity of the creature, the greater by the work of God is the advantage to the soul. While the human instrument strives to do harm, the Divine Workman in whose hands the soul is, makes use of the very malice to remove from the soul all that might be prejudicial to it.

The will of God has nothing but sweetness, favors, and treasures for submissive souls; it is impossible to repose too much confidence in it, nor to abandon oneself to it too utterly. It always acts for and desires that which is most conducive to our perfection, provided we allow it to act. Faith does not doubt. The more unfaithful, uncertain, and rebellious are the senses, the louder faith cries: "All is well; it is the will of God." There is nothing that the eye of faith does not penetrate, nothing that the power of faith does not overcome. It passes through the thick darkness and no matter what clouds may gather, it goes straight to the truth and, holding to it firmly, will never let it go.

— Excerpt from *Abandonment to Divine Providence*,
Book 1: Chapter 2, Section 2.

# VI

# The Will of God

The divine action places before us at every moment things of infinite value and gives them to us according to the measure of our faith and love.

If we understood how to see in each moment some manifestation of the will of God, we should find therein also all that our hearts could desire. In fact there could be nothing more reasonable, more perfect, more divine than the will of God. Could any change of time, place, or circumstance alter or increase its infinite value? If you possess the secret of discovering the will of God at every moment and in everything, then you possess all that is most precious and most worthy to be desired. What is it that you desire, you who aim at perfection? Give yourselves full scope. Your wishes need have no measure, no limit. However much you may desire I can show you how to attain it, even though it be infinite. There is never a moment in which I cannot enable you to obtain all that you can want. The present is ever filled with infinite treasure. It contains more than you have the capacity to hold. Faith is the measure. Believe and it will be done to you accordingly. Love also is the measure. The more the heart loves, the more it desires; and the more it desires, so much the more will it receive. The will of God is at each moment before us like an immense, inexhaustible ocean that no human heart can fathom; but none can receive from it more than he has the capacity to contain. It is necessary to enlarge this capacity by faith, confidence, and love.

The whole creation cannot fill the human heart, for the heart is greater than all that is not God. It is on a higher plane than the material creation and for this reason nothing material can satisfy it. The divine will is a deep abyss of which the present moment is the entrance. If you plunge into this abyss you will find it infinitely more vast than your desires. Do not flatter anyone, nor worship your own illusions. They can neither give you anything nor receive anything from you. Receive your fullness from the will of God alone, it will not leave you empty. Adore it, put it first before all things; tear all disguises from vain pretenses and forsake them all, going straight to the sole reality. The reign of faith is death to the senses; it is their spoliation, their destruction. The senses worship creatures; faith adores the divine will. Destroy the idols of the senses and they will rebel and lament, but faith must triumph because the will of God is indestructible. When the senses are terrified or famished, despoiled or crushed, then it is that faith is nourished, enriched, and enlivened. Faith laughs at these calamities as a governor of an impregnable fortress laughs at the useless attacks of an impotent foe. When a soul recognizes the will of God and shows a readiness to submit to it entirely, then God gives himself to such a soul and renders it most powerful succor under all circumstances. Thus it experiences a great happiness in this advent of God and enjoys it the more, the more it has learned to abandon itself at every moment to his adorable will.

— Excerpt from *Abandonment to Divine Providence*,
Book 1: Chapter 2: Section 3.

# VII

# Love's Hidden Work

The divine love is communicated to us through every creature under a veil, as in the eucharistic species.

What great truths are hidden even from Christians who imagine themselves most enlightened! How many are there among them who understand that every cross, every action, every attraction according to the designs of God gives God to us. Could there be any better way of explaining this than through a comparison with the most august mystery of the Eucharist? Nevertheless, there is nothing more certain. For does not reason as well as faith reveal to us the real presence of divine love in all creatures and in all the events of life, as indubitably as the words of

Jesus Christ and the Church reveal that the sacred Body and Blood of our Savior are present in the Eucharist? Do we not know that by all creatures and by every event the divine love desires to unite us to himself, that he has ordained, arranged, or permitted everything in our regard, everything that happens to us with a view to this union? This is the ultimate object of all his designs, and to attain it he makes use of all his creatures, the worst as well as the best, and uses the most distressing events as well as those which are pleasant and agreeable.

Our communion with him is even more meritorious when the means that serve to bring it about are repugnant to nature. If this be true, every moment of our lives may be a kind of communion with the divine love, and this communion of every moment may produce as much fruit in our souls as that which we receive in the communion of the Body and Blood of the Son of God. This latter, it is true, is efficacious sacramentally which the former cannot be. Nevertheless, how much more frequently can this communion of every moment be renewed and what great increase of merit can it achieve when it is accomplished with perfect dispositions. Consequently, how true it is that the more holy the life the more mysterious it becomes by its apparent simplicity and littleness. O great feast! O perpetual festival! God! Given and received under all that is most feeble, foolish, and worthless upon earth! God chooses that which nature abhors and human prudence rejects. Of these he makes mysteries, sacraments of love. And through that which potentially could do the most harm to souls, God gives himself to them as often and as much as the soul desires to possess him.

— Excerpt from *Abandonment to Divine Providence*,
Book 1: Chapter 2, Section 7.

# VIII

# The Present Moment

O all you who thirst, learn that you have not far to go to find the fountain of living waters; it flows quite close to you in the present moment. Therefore, hasten to find it. Why, with the fountain so near, do you tire yourselves with running about after every little rill? These only increase your thirst by providing you with only a few drops, whereas the source is inexhaustible. If you desire to think, to write, and to speak like the prophets, the apostles, and the saints, you must give yourself up as they did to the inspirations of God. O unknown Love! It seems as if your wonders were finished and nothing remained but to copy your ancient works and to quote your past discourses! And no one sees that your inexhaustible activity is a source of new thoughts, of fresh sufferings and further actions: of new patriarchs, apostles, prophets, and saints who have no need to copy the lives and writings of the others, but only to live in perpetual abandonment to your secret operations. We hear of nothing on all sides but "the first centuries," "the time of the saints." What a strange way of talking! Do we not realize that God works in every moment, filling and sanctifying them, giving them each a supernatural quality? Has there ever been an ancient method of abandonment to God's operation which fell out of season? Had the saints of the first ages any other secret than that of becoming from moment to moment whatever the divine power willed to make them? And will this power cease to pour forth its glory on the souls that abandon themselves to it without reserve?

O Love eternal, adorable, ever fruitful and ever marvelous! May the divine operation of my God be my book, my doctrine, my science. In it are my thoughts, my words, my actions, and my sufferings. Not by consulting your former works shall I become what you would have me to be, but by receiving you in everything. By that ancient road, the only royal road, the road of our fathers, shall I be enlightened and shall speak as they spoke. It is thus that I would imitate them all, quote them all, copy them all.

— Excerpt from *Abandonment to Divine Providence*, Book 1: Chapter 2, Section 9.

# IX

# Allow God to Act

It is necessary to be detached from all that one feels and from all that one does if one would follow this method by which one lives in God alone and in one's present duty. All regard to what is beyond this should be cut off as superfluous. One must keep one's attention on the present duty, not bothering with what has gone before or what duties the future will bring.

In the state of abandonment, the only rule is the duty of the present moment. In this the soul is light as a feather, fluid as water, simple as a child, active as a ball in receiving and following all the inspirations of grace. Such souls are not rigid, but like molten metal take the form of the mold into which they are poured, so these souls are easily receptive of any form that God chooses to give them. In a word, their disposition resembles the air which goes willingly where it is stirred by every breeze; or water which flows into vessels of any shape, filling them completely. Before God they are like a clean, smooth canvas waiting for the artist's brush; they neither think nor seek to know what God will be pleased to trace thereon, because they have such confidence in him. They abandon themselves to God and, entirely absorbed by their duty, they think not of themselves, nor of what may be necessary for them, nor of how to obtain it. The more assiduously do they apply themselves to their little work, so simple, so hidden, so secret and outwardly contemptible, the more does God embroider and embellish it with brilliant colors. On the surface of this simple canvas of love and obedience his hand traces the most beautiful design, the most delicate and intricate pattern, the most divine figures. "The LORD hath made his holy one wonderful"—"*Mirificavit Dominus sanctum suum*" (Ps 4:4 *Douay Rheims*).

It is true that a canvas simply and blindly given up to the brush's strokes only feels the movement of the brush at each moment. It is the same with a sculpture. The stone gives itself up to the blow of the hammer and chisel which produce one cruel mark at a time. The stone struck by repeated blows cannot know nor see the form produced by them. It only feels—if it could—that it is being diminished, filed, cut, and altered by the chisel. And if a stone destined by the sculptor to become a beautiful crucifix or a statue were asked, "What is happening to you?" it would reply, if it could speak, "Do not ask me! I only know one thing and that is that I must remain immovable in the hands of my master. I must love him and to endure all that he inflicts upon me. As for the end for which I am destined, it is his business to understand how it is to be accomplished. I am as ignorant of what he is doing as of what I am destined to become. All I know is that his work is the best and the most perfect that could be, and I receive each blow of the chisel as the most excellent thing that could happen to me, although, truth to tell, each blow, in my opinion, is ruining me, destroying me, disfiguring me. But this is not my affair. Content with the present moment I think of nothing but my duty, and I endure the work of this clever master without knowing or occupying myself about it."

Allow God to act, and abandon yourself to him. Let the chisel perform its office, the needle do its work. Let the brush of the artist cover the canvas with many tints which only have the appearance of daubs. Correspond with all these divine operations by a simple and constant submission, a forgetfulness of self and an assiduous application to duty. Continue thus in your own groove without studying the way, the ins and outs, the surroundings, the names or particulars of the places. Go on blindly pursuing this path and you will be shown what is to follow. Seek only the kingdom of God and his justice by love and obedience and all the rest will be added to you. We meet with many souls who are distressed about themselves and inquire anxiously, "Who will direct us so that we may become mortified and holy and attain perfection?" Let them search in books for the description and characteristics of this marvelous work, its nature and qualities; but as for you, remain peacefully united to God by love and follow blindly the clear straight path of duty. The angels are at your side during this time of darkness and they will bear you up. If God requires more of you, he will make it known to you by his inspirations.

— Excerpt from *Abandonment to Divine Providence*,
Book 2: Chapter 2, Section 6.

# X

# Trust in God

When God makes himself the guide of a soul, he exacts from it an absolute confidence in him and a freedom from any sort of disquietude as to the way in which he conducts it. This soul, therefore, is urged on without perceiving the path traced out before it. It does not imitate either what it has seen, or what it has read, but proceeds by its own action and cannot do otherwise without grave risk. The divine action is ever fresh, it never retraces its steps, but always marks out new ways. Souls that are conducted by it never know where they are going; their ways are neither to be found in books, nor in their own minds; the divine action carries them step by step and they progress only according to its movement.

When you are conducted by a guide who takes you through an unknown country at night across fields where there are no tracks, by his own skill, without asking advice from anyone, or giving you any inkling of his plans, how can you choose but to abandon yourself? Of what use is it looking about to find out where you are, to ask the passersby, or to consult maps and travelers? The plans or fancies of a guide who insists on being trusted would not allow this. He would take pleasure in overcoming the anxiety and distrust of the soul and would insist on an entire surrender to his guidance. If one is convinced that he is a good guide, one must have faith in him and abandon oneself to his care.

The divine action is essentially good; it does not need to be reformed or controlled. It began at the creation of the world, and to the present time has manifested ever fresh energy. Its operations are without limit, its fecundity inexhaustible. It acted in one way yesterday, today it acts differently. It is the same action applied at each moment to produce ever new effects and it will extend from eternity to eternity. It has produced Abel, Noah, Abraham, all three of whom are different types; Isaac, also original, and Jacob from no copy; neither does Joseph follow any prefigure. Moses has no prototype among his progenitors. David and the prophets are quite different from the patriarchs. Saint John the Baptist stands alone. Jesus Christ is the firstborn; the apostles act more by the guidance of his spirit than in imitation of his works.

Jesus Christ did not set a limit for himself, neither did he follow all his own maxims to the letter. The Holy Spirit ever inspired his holy soul, and being entirely abandoned to the Spirit's every breath, he had no need to consult the moment that had passed, to know how to act in that which was coming. The breath of grace shaped every moment according to the eternal truths subsisting in the invisible and unfathomable wisdom of the Blessed Trinity. The soul of Jesus Christ received these directions at every moment and acted upon them.

The Gospel shows in the life of Jesus Christ a succession of these truths; and this same Jesus who lives and works always, continues to live and work in the souls of his saints.

— Excerpt from *Abandonment to Divine Providence*,
Book 2: Chapter 2, Section 7.

# XI

# Given Over to God

It seems to me that it is easy to conclude from all this that souls abandoned to God cannot occupy themselves, as others do, with desires, examinations, cares, or attachments to certain persons. Neither can they form plans, nor lay down methodical rules for their actions, or for reading. This would imply that they still had power to dispose of themselves, which would entirely exclude the state of abandonment in which they are placed. In this state they give up to God all their rights over themselves, over their words, actions, thoughts, and proceedings, over the employment of their time and everything connected with it. There remains only one desire, to satisfy the Master they have chosen, to listen unceasingly to the expression of his will in order to execute it immediately. No condition can better represent this state than that of a servant who obeys every order he receives and does not occupy his time in attending to his own affairs; these he neglects in order to serve his Master at every moment. These souls then should not be distressed at their powerlessness; they are able to do much in being able to give themselves entirely to a Master who is all-powerful and able to work wonders with the feeblest of instruments if they offer no resistance.

Let us, then, endure without annoyance the humiliations brought on us, in our own eyes and in the eyes of others, by what shows outwardly in our lives; or rather, let us conceal ourselves behind these outward appearances and enjoy God who is all ours. Let us profit by this apparent failure, by these requirements, by this need to be cared for, and the necessity of constant nourishment and of comfort, of our lack of success, of the contempt of others, of these fears, uncertainties, troubles, etc., to find all our wealth and happiness in God, who by these means, gives himself entirely to us as our only good. God wishes to be ours in a poor way, without all those accessories of sanctity which make others to be admired, and this is because God would be himself the sole food of our souls, the only object of our desires. We are so weak that if we displayed the virtues of zeal, almsgiving, poverty, and austerity, we should make them subjects for vainglory. But as it is, everything is disagreeable in order that God may be our whole sanctification, our whole support, so that the world despises us and leaves us to enjoy our treasure in peace. God desires to be the principle of all that is holy in us and, therefore, what depends on ourselves and on our active fidelity is very small and appears quite contrary to sanctity. There cannot be anything great in us in the sight of God except our total receptivity to his will. Therefore, let us think of it no more. Let us leave the care of our sanctification to God who well knows how to bring it about. It all depends on the watchful care and particular operation of Divine Providence and is accomplished in a great measure without our knowledge and even in a way that is unexpected and disagreeable to us. Let us fulfill peacefully the little duties of our active fidelity, without aspiring to those that are greater, because God does not give himself to us by reason of our own efforts. We shall become saints of God, of his grace, and of his special providence. He knows what rank to give us, let us leave it to him and without forming to ourselves false ideas and empty systems of sanctity, let us content ourselves with loving him unceasingly and in pursuing with simplicity the path he has marked out for us, where all is so mean and paltry in our eyes and in the estimation of the world.

— Excerpt from *Abandonment to Divine Providence*,
Book 2: Chapter 3, Section 3.

# XII

# All-Sufficient Love

While despoiling of all things those souls who give themselves entirely to him, God gives them something in place of them. Instead of light, wisdom, life, and strength, he gives them his love. The divine love in these souls is like a supernatural instinct. In nature, each thing contains that which is suitable to its kind. Each flower has its special beauty, each animal its instinct, and each creature its perfection. Also in the different states of grace, each has a special grace. This is the recompense for everyone who accepts with goodwill the state in which he is placed by Providence. A soul comes under the divine action from the moment that a habit of goodwill is formed within it, and this action influences it more or less according to its degree of abandonment. The whole art of abandonment is simply that of loving, and the divine action is nothing else than the action of divine love. How can it be that these two loves seeking each other should do otherwise than unite when they meet? How can the divine love refuse anything to a soul whose every desire it directs. And how can a soul that lives only for him refuse him anything? Love can refuse nothing that love desires, nor desire anything that love refuses. The divine action regards only the goodwill; the capability of the other faculties does not attract it, nor does the want of capability repel it. All that it requires is a heart that is good, pure, just, simple, submissive, filial, and respectful. It takes possession of such a heart and of all its faculties, and so arranges everything for its benefit that it finds in all things its sanctification. That which destroys other souls would find in this soul an antidote of goodwill which would nullify its poison. Even at the edge of a precipice the divine action would draw it back, or even if it were allowed to remain there it would prevent it from falling; and if it fell, it would rescue it. After all, the faults of such a soul are only faults of frailty; love takes but little notice of them, and well knows how to turn them to advantage. It makes the soul understand by secret suggestions what it ought to say, or to do, according to circumstances. If they make arrangements which would involve them in some promise prejudicial to them, Divine Providence arranges some fortunate occurrence which recitifes everything. In vain are schemes formed against them repeatedly; Divine Providence cuts all the knots, brings the authors to confusion, and so turns their heads as to make them fall into their own trap. Under its guidance those souls that they wish to take by surprise do certain things that seem very useless at the time, but that serve afterward to deliver them from all the troubles into which their uprightness and the malice of their enemies would have plunged them. Oh! What good policy it is to have goodwill! What prudence there is in simplicity! What good fortune in its innocence and candor! What mysteries and secrets in its straightforwardness! . . .

Divine love, then, is to those who give themselves up to it without reserve, the principle of all good. To acquire this inestimable treasure the only thing necessary is greatly to desire it. Yes, God only asks for love, and if you seek this treasure, this kingdom in which God reigns alone, you will find it.

That all things work for its good is an article of faith.

— Excerpt from *Abandonment to Divine Providence*,
Book 2: Chapter 4, Section 9.

# XIII

# Peace in Turmoil

What I have always feared has come to pass. I have no power to refuse a charge that is contrary to all my predilections and for which I do not believe myself to have any aptitude. In vain have I groaned, prayed, implored, and even offered to remain all my life in the vicariate of Toulouse: I have been compelled to make the sacrifice—one of the greatest of my whole life. But now I see plainly the hand of Providence. The sacrifice having been made and reiterated a hundred times, God has taken from me all my former repugnance, so that I left the motherhouse, which you know how much I loved, with a peace and liberty of spirit which astonished even me. More still! When

I arrived at Perpignan I found a large amount of business to attend to, none of which I understood; and many people to see and to deal with: the Bishop, the steward, the king's lieutenant, the Parliament, the garrison staff. You know what horror I have always entertained for visits of any sort and above all for those of grand people. Well! None of these have given me any alarm; in God I hope to find a remedy for everything, and I feel a confidence in Divine Providence which enables me to surmount all difficulties.

Besides this I enjoy peace and tranquility in the midst of a thousand cares and anxieties, which I should have imagined would have naturally overwhelmed me. It is true that what most contributes to produce this great peace is that God has rendered my soul impervious to fear, and I desire nothing for this short and miserable life. Therefore, when I have done all in my power or which I felt before God I ought to do, I leave the rest to him, abandoning everything entirely and with my whole heart to Divine Providence, blessing him beforehand for all things and wishing in all and above all that his holy will be done. I am convinced by faith and by numerous personal experiences that all comes from God, and that he is so powerful and such a good Father that he will cause everything to prosper for the advantage of his dear children. Has he not proved that he loves us more than life itself. . . ? Therefore, since he has done so much for love of us, are we not convinced that he will not forget us? I entreat you, then, not to worry about me and my affairs. Do the same that I have constrained myself to do. Once I have taken measures before God and according to his will, I leave all the rest to him and look to him for success. I wait for this success with confidence, but also in peace; and whatever takes place I accept, not for the satisfaction of my impatient desires, but keeping pace with Divine Providence, who rules and arranges all for our greater good, although generally we do not understand any of his ways. And how can we dare to judge him, poor ignorant creatures as we are who are blind as the moles that burrow underground.

Let us accept all from the hand of our good Father, and he will keep us in peace in the midst of the greatest disasters of this world, which pass away like shadows. In proportion to our abandonment and confidence in God will our lives be holy and tranquil. Also where this abandonment is neglected there can be no virtue, nor any perfect rest.

— Excerpt from a letter written to
Sister Marie Thérèse de Vioménil. Perpignan, 1740.

# XIV

# Liberty of Spirit

I am touched by your desire to share in my trials, but I am happy in being able to reassure you. It is true that, at first, I felt a keen pain at finding myself loaded with a multitude of business affairs and other cares quite contrary to my attraction for silence and solitude; but notice how Divine Providence has arranged things.

God has given me the grace not to attach myself to any of these affairs; therefore, my spirit is always at liberty. I recommend the success of them to his Fatherly care, and this is why nothing distresses me. Things often go perfectly and then I return thanks to God for it, but sometimes everything goes wrong, and I bless him for that equally and offer it to him as a sacrifice. Once this sacrifice is made God puts everything right. Already this good Master has, more than once, given me these pleasant surprises. As regards having time to myself, I have more here than elsewhere. Visits are rare now, because I only go where duty obliges me or necessity calls me. God has given me the grace not to care how discontented people are with me for following my own bent. It is he alone who we ought to have any great interest in pleasing. As long as he is satisfied, that is enough for us all; other things are a mere nothing. In a short time we shall appear before this great and sovereign Master, this Infinite Being. Alas! Of what avail will it be to us then for eternity to have done anything except for him and inspired by his grace and his Holy Spirit? If one becomes more familiar with these simple truths, what repose would not our hearts and souls enjoy during this present life? From how many idle fears, foolish desires, and useless anxieties should we not be delivered—not only concerning this life, but also the next? I assure you that since my return to France I begin to look forward more than ever with great peace and tranquility to the end of this sad life. How could I experience aught but joy at seeing the end of my exile approaching?

— Excerpt from an undated letter to an unknown recipient.

# XV

# Recourse to Providence

I am constantly experiencing here the action of Divine Providence, for no sooner do I make a sacrifice of everything to him than he rectifies the situation and makes all turn out for the best. When I find myself at the last resource I place all my needs in the hands of that good Providence from whom I hope all things. I have recourse to him always. I thank him without ceasing for all, accepting all from his divine hand. Never does he fail those who put their whole trust in his protection. On the other hand, how do people usually act? They substitute themselves, blind and powerless as they are, for that Divine Providence which is infinitely wise and infinitely good. They build on their own efforts, and thus withdrawing themselves from the ruling of divine love, they deprive themselves of the help they would have received had they kept within its shelter. What folly! How can we doubt that God understands our requirements better than we do ourselves and that his arrangements in our regard are most advantageous to us although we do not comprehend them?

We might make use of the small amount of sense we possess to decide that we will allow ourselves to be guided by that sweet Providence even though we cannot fathom the secret activities it employs, nor the particular ends it desires to attain. Should you remark, "If it is sufficient for us passively to submit to be led then what about the proverb 'God helps those who help themselves'?" I would answer, "I did not say you were to do nothing—without doubt it is necessary to help ourselves. Indeed, to wait with folded arms for everything to drop from heaven is a natural inclination, but this would be an absurd and culpable quietism applied to supernatural graces." Therefore, while cooperating with God and leaning on him, you yourself must never leave off working. To act in this way is to act with certainty and consequently with calmness. When, in all our actions we look upon ourselves as instruments in the hands of God, to work out his hallowed designs, we shall act quietly, without anxiety, without hurry, without uneasiness about the future; without troubling about the past, giving ourselves up to the fatherly providence of God and relying more on him than on all possible human means. In this way, we shall always be at peace and God will infallibly turn everything to our good, whether temporal or eternal.

— Excerpt from a letter written to
Sister Marie Thérèse de Vioménil. Perpignan, 1741.

# XVI

# Dependence on God

D o not ask me for new ways of acquiring the friend-ship of God and of making rapid progress in virtue. I know only one way which I have more than once explained to you and the infallible efficacy of which my daily experience demonstrates more and more clearly. This secret is abandonment to Divine Providence. Bear with me for calling your attention to it once again and do not grow weary, either, of learning what I do not weary of teaching you. I should like to cry out everywhere, "Aban-donment! Abandonment!" and again "Abandonment!" unbounded and unreserved; and for two good reasons.

First, because the greatness of God and his sovereign dominion over all, require that all creatures should bow before him, that all should be cast down and as it were annihilated before his Supreme Majesty. There is no comparison between his infinite greatness and our nothingness. It is above all things, comprehends all things, absorbs all things in its immensity. Or, rather, it *is* all things since all things that have a separate existence from the Divinity have received their being from him in creation and still continue to receive it in their preservation which is the unceasing renewal of creation. Thus the existence we have received from God remains, as it were, in the bosom of the Divinity and never leaves its service, but remains plunged and engulfed therein. God, then, is the author of all being. Nothing is, nor lives, nor subsists, nor moves, but by him and in him. He is Who Is, the One by Whom and in Whom all exists and Who is in all things.

Things, compared with nothingness, seem to have an existence, but, compared with God, they are nothing. They only possess being and substance by the gift of God, while he alone exists of himself and owes nothing to any other than himself. Therefore, as everything belongs to him, necessarily everything will return to him in order that his supreme dominion may be glorified by all his creatures. Those creatures that do not have the gift of reason glorify him according to their state by following with complete exactness and perfect obedience the laws of their nature. But God has a right to expect from his reasonable creatures a glory far more worthy of him, which results from their voluntary abandonment. And what more just and noble use could any reasonable creature make of its liberty than in rendering to God all it has received from him, and in offering him in advance all that may be added to it in the future? Understand me thoroughly: God alone can give us the power of rendering the homage he expects from us by arousing in us the thought, the desire, and the will to do so. Moreover, if God gives us this grace and if we profit by it, far from taking the credit to ourselves we ought to thank him for it as the crown of all his other benefits. The very impulse that prompts us to offer up this thanksgiving is the fruit of yet another grace. . . . Thus, each of our moments, each of our actions, in increasing our debt, forms new ties and makes us depend more entirely on the divine goodness. At this thought, our spirit, our heart, our soul remain as though engulfed, lost, abandoned into the profound abyss of his sovereign dominion. . . .

The second motive to induce us to abandon ourselves without reserve is, that, unless God receives from his creatures the homage due to his Infinite Majesty he cannot give free vent to his infinite goodness. All that his creatures bring to him by a total renunciation, he wills to return to them by a gratuitous gift of his mercy; or rather, he repays infinitely more than they have given him, because in return for the gift of their limited being he bestows on them his infinite riches. Therefore at the bottom of this abyss of renunciation where we should expect to find nothingness, we find infinitude. What an exchange of the divine liberality! What ingenuity of divine wisdom! What a surprise of the divine goodness brings about for us!

— Excerpt from a letter written to
Sister Marie-Anne Thérèse de Rosen, 1724.

# XVII

# The Goodness of God

I do not understand your uneasiness, my dear Sister, nor why you take pleasure in tormenting yourself as you do about the future, when your faith teaches you that the future is in the hands of an infinitely good Father who loves you more than you love yourself and who understands what is necessary for you much better than you do yourself. Have you forgotten that everything that happens is ordained by Divine Providence? And if we recognize this truth how is it that we are not humbly submissive in every event both great and small to all that God wills or permits?

Oh! How blind we are when we desire anything other than what God wills! He alone knows the dangers that threaten us in the future and the help we shall require. I am strongly persuaded that we should all be lost if God were to grant us all that we asked for. This is why, says Saint Augustine, God, out of compassion for our blindness, does not always hear our prayers and often gives us the exact contrary of what we asked him, as being in truth better for us. Truly, it seems to me that in this world nearly all of us are like people who in madness or delirium ask for exactly what will cause their death and to whom it is refused out of charity or in pity. Oh my God! If this truth were but understood, with what blind abandonment would we not submit to all the decrees of your Divine Providence! What peace and tranquility of heart should we enjoy about all things and in all things, not only as to outward events but also about the interior state of our soul. Even if the painful vicissitudes through which God makes us pass should be in punishment for our unfaithfulness, we ought to say to ourselves, "God wills it by permitting it," and humbly submit. We must then detest the offense and accept the painful and humiliating consequences, as Saint Francis de Sales so often recommends. Would that this principle, thoroughly grasped, could put an end to the troubles and anxieties that are so useless and so destructive of our peace of mind and spiritual progress. Shall I never be able even with the help of grace to introduce into your soul this great principle of faith, so sweet, so consoling, so tranquilizing? "Oh my God!" we ought to repeat, "may your will be accomplished in me and never my own. May yours be accomplished because it is infinitely just and also infinitely advantageous to me. I acknowledge that you can will nothing that is not for the greatest benefit to your creatures as long as they are submissive to your commands. May my wishes never be granted if they do not agree perfectly with yours, because in that case they would be disastrous to me. And if even, my God, it happens that either through ignorance or passion I should persist in desiring things contrary to your will, may I always be refused or punished, as the result, not of your justice, but of your compassion and great mercy."

"Whatever happens," said Saint Francis de Sales, "I shall always side with Divine Providence, even if human wisdom tears her hair out with spite." If you were more enlightened you would judge very differently from the ordinary run of human beings. What a source of peace and strength this way of looking at things would prove for you. How happy are the saints! And how peacefully they live! And how blind and stupid we are in not accustoming ourselves to think and act as they do, but to prefer living shut up in thick darkness which makes us wretched as well as blind and guilty. Let us then make it our study, aim, and purpose to conform ourselves in all things to the holy will of God in spite of interior rebellion. Even about this rebellion we must acquiesce in the will of God for it compels us to remain always before him in a state of sacrifice as to all things; in an interior silence of respect, adoration, self-effacement, submission, love, and an entire abandonment full of confidence to his divine will.

— Excerpt from an undated letter written to
Sister Marie Thérèse de Vioménil.

# XVIII

# Annoyances

The annoyances you have experienced must have been all the more painful as they came from people from whom you would have least expected them; but be assured that you will have gained great merit for heaven by them. People's ideas are so different; they vary according to their interests or temper and each is convinced of his own sense and that he has right on his side. Oh men! Men! To what have we come? What an abyss of humiliation for the whole human race! It is a good thing to have arrived at the bottom of this abyss, for it will be easier to place all one's confidence in God. The mind, enlightened by faith, disposes the heart to submit to the decrees of

Divine Providence who permits good people to make each other suffer to detach them from each other. On occasions such as these we can only resign ourselves and abandon ourselves to God who will support us. These dispositions will enable us to turn a deaf ear to arguments that might tend to disturb us. Whether we consider ourselves or the conduct of others toward us, there will never be wanting specious reasons for becoming vexed and uneasy. But there is never any reason for depression and worry. These irregular emotions are always contrary to reason as well as to religion; and the peace of which they deprive us is of incalculably more value than that for which we sacrifice it.

For the rest it is always allowable to speak in confidence to a director, to obtain consolation, strength, and instruction, but always do so with charity and discretion. Nevertheless, it is better and more perfect to keep silence. It is to God alone that we should confide our vexations and tell all as to a friend or director worthy of our entire confidence. This is an excellent and easy way of praying and is called the prayer of confidence and the outpouring of the heart before God. By it is gained great spiritual fortitude and from it proceeds consolation, peace, and courage. If you continue to live as you are doing now, very imperfectly no doubt, but with a sincere desire to improve, and with efforts proportioned to your weakness, your salvation is certain. Even the fear you feel about it is a gift of God provided it does not go so far as to trouble you and to prevent you frequenting the sacraments, practicing virtue, or continuing your spiritual exercises. As for the hardness of heart and want of feeling that you complain about, be patient and offer this affliction to God in a spirit of penance as you offer him your illnesses and bodily infirmities. Those of the soul are much harder to bear and consequently more meritorious.

— Excerpt from an undated letter written to
Sister Marie Thérèse de Vioménil.

# XIX

## How to Bear Trials

I feel keenly, my dear Sister, the painful nature of the trial to which God has subjected you and the sadness of your heart at receiving these daily wounds.

It is true, I own, that it is necessary to be very holy to be able to let such things pass unnoticed, without feeling any kind of resentment. However, if you cannot attain such perfection at least try during these times of trial, first, to dismiss as far as you are able all those thoughts, feelings, and that language likely to embitter your mind, and, second, if you cannot succeed in doing this, at any rate, say interiorly in the superior part of your soul, "My God, you have permitted this, may your adorable will and divine decrees be accomplished in all things. I sacrifice to you this affliction and its consequences according to what pleases you. You are the Master, may you be blessed by all and in all things." Then add, "I forgive, Lord, from the bottom of my heart for the love of you the persons who cause my sufferings, and to show the sincerity of my feelings about them, I ask for them all sorts of graces and blessings and every happiness." When the heart is inclined to resist say, "My God, you see my misery, but at least I desire to have all these feelings and I beg this grace of you." Having done this think no more about it, and if uncharitable feelings still attack you, be resigned to endure this torment in conformity to the divine will which permits it, contenting yourself with renewing your offering in the higher part of the soul. This is one of the ways by which we can share the chalice of Jesus Christ, our Good Master.

---

I am surprised, my dear Sister, that with the help of the rules I have so often given you, you are not even yet able to recognize the hand of God in the misunderstandings that arise among people with the best intentions. "God," you say, "does not inspire anything that brings trouble." That, in one sense, is true, but is it not also true that God has permitted, and often permits his servants to be given to mistakes and illusions which are intended to try them, to exercise them, and, in this way to sanctify them by the trouble they cause each other? We see hundreds of examples of this in the lives of the saints. . . . Try to judge, not by human judgment, weak, narrow, and blind as it is, but by divine judgment which alone is upright, sure, and infallible. In this way you will improve, and not have the peace of your mind and heart disturbed.

— Excerpt from two undated letters written to
Sister Marie Thérèse de Vioménil.

# XX

# Why Torment Yourself?

Believe me, my dear Sister, and put an end to all your fears and entrust all to Divine Providence who makes use of hidden but infallible means of bringing everything to serve his ends. Whatever others may say or do, they can only act by God's will or permission, and everything they do he makes serve the accomplishment of his merciful designs. He is able to attain his purposes by means apparently most contrary, as to refresh his servants in the midst of a fiery furnace or to make them walk on the waters. We shall experience more sensibly this fatherly protection of Providence if we abandon ourselves to him with filial confidence. Quite recently I have had experience of this.

Therefore, I have prayed to God with greater fervor than ever to grant me the grace never to have my own will, which is always blind and often dangerous, but always that his will, which is just, holy, loving, and beneficent may be accomplished. Ah! If you only knew what a pleasure it is to find no peace or contentment except in accomplishing the will of God, which is as good as it is powerful, you would not be able to desire anything else. Never look upon any pain, no matter of what kind, as a sign of being far from God; because crosses and sufferings are, on the contrary, effects of his goodness and love. "But," you say, "what will become of me if . . . ?" This is indeed a temptation of the enemy. Why should you be so ingenious in tormenting yourself beforehand about something which perhaps will never happen? Sufficient for the day is the evil thereof. Uneasy forebodings do us much harm; why do you so readily give way to them? We make our own troubles and what do we gain by it? Rather we lose so much both for time and eternity. When we are obsessed in spite of ourselves by these worrying anticipations let us be faithful in making a continual offering of them to the sovereign Master. I beg you to do this, as in this way you will induce God to deal favorably with you and to help you in every way. You will acquire a treasure of virtue and merits for heaven and a submission and abandonment which will enable you to make more progress in the ways of God

than any other practice of piety. It is possible for this purpose that God permits all these troublesome and trying
imaginations. Profit by them then and God will bless you.
By your submission to his good pleasure you will make
greater progress than you could by hearing beautiful ser-
mons or reading pious books. If you only understood this
great truth thoroughly, you would enjoy great peace of
mind and advance rapidly in the ways of God. Without
this submission to his good pleasure, no spirituality counts
for much. As long as people restrict themselves to exterior
practices, they can but have a very thin veneer of true and
solid piety which essentially consists in willing in all things
what God wills and in the manner in which he wills it.
When you have attained to this, the Spirit of God will
reign absolutely in your heart, will supply for all else, and
will never fail you in your need if you call with humble
confidence for his help. This is faith, but is known to very
few souls who are otherwise pious. Thus, for the want of
this disposition we see them kept back and obstructed in
the ways of God. What a pitiful blindness! All the business
and complicated affairs in which we are immersed by
God's will and by the decrees of his Divine Providence,
are equal to the most delightful contemplation, if one says
from the bottom of one's heart, "My God, this is your will,
and, therefore, also mine." Although this is said only in the
higher part of the soul without the will seeming to take

any share in it, still the offering is no less agreeable to God and meritorious for oneself. Keep with a firm determination to this practice and you will soon experience its excellent results. If you could also combine with it a certain peace and quietness of mind, a certain gentleness of manner toward others and also toward yourself, without ever showing signs of annoyance, worry, or vexation, what great and meritorious sacrifices you will have made!

— Excerpt from an undated letter written to Sister Marie Thérèse de Vioménil.

# XXI

# The Happiness of Resignation

It does not astonish me, my dear Sister, that you find it difficult to understand the ways of Divine Providence. Neither do I understand them any better than you, but what I know and what you know as well as I, is that God arranges and disposes of all things as he pleases and makes use of who he will, to carry out his designs at the time and moment he has decided upon. Let us learn then to resign ourselves in all and everything with submission and confidence in he who can do all things and who disposes of all things according to his own plans. If we could only attain to this state of holy submission we should wait patiently for things to happen at the appointed time, instead of at the time that, in our impatience, we expect them. Abandonment to God's holy Providence binds him, in a way, to find a remedy for everything and to provide for and console us in all our needs. Remind yourself of this great saying, "Everything passes away, God alone remains." Abandon yourself and all who are dear to you, therefore, to his loving care. In public disasters as in all other things we should, by our confidence, glorify his infinite goodness and then we shall be able to say with David: "We have rejoiced for the days in which thou hast humbled us: for the years in which we have seen evils" (Ps 89:15 *Douay Rheims*). Suffering, patiently endured, is the lot and the seal of the elect; let us say also with the same prophet, "I was dumb, and I opened not my mouth, because thou hast done it" (Ps 38:10 *Douay Rheims*). There is no greater consolation in our trials than a lively faith in the goodness of him who sends them, an expectation of that eternal happiness these trials have merited for us, the remembrance of our sins that they help to expiate, and the contemplation of the sufferings that Jesus Christ underwent for love of us. Impatience would only serve to aggravate the evil, while patience has the great power of lightening them. God has different rods with which he threatens us and punishes our sins, but always with a fatherly love, since he only threatens and punishes us in this world in order to be able to save us with greater certainty. May he be blessed forever!

— Excerpt from an undated letter written
to an unnamed sister.

# XXII

# Peace and Confidence

What you tell me about the peace and tranquility you experience has given me great pleasure. You must remember all your life that one of the principal reasons why certain souls do not advance is because the devil continually throws them in to a state of uneasiness, perplexity, and anxiety, which makes them incapable of applying themselves seriously, quietly, and with constancy to the practice of virtue. The great principle of the interior life is this peace of soul and it must be preserved with such care, that the moment it is attacked all else must be put aside and every effort made to try and regain this holy peace, just as, in an outbreak of fire everything else is neglected to hasten to extinguish the flames . . .

Peace and tranquility of mind alone give great strength to the soul, to enable it to do all that God wishes, while, on the other hand, anxiety and uneasiness make the soul feeble and languid as though sick. Then one feels neither taste for, nor attraction to, virtue; but, on the contrary, disgust and discouragement, of which the devil does not fail to take advantage. For this reason he uses all his pretexts, at one time about self-examination or sorrow for sin, at another about the way we continually neglect grace, or that by our own fault we make no progress; that God will, at last, forsake us and a hundred other devices from which very few people can defend themselves. This is why masters of the spiritual life lay down this great principle to distinguish the true inspirations of God from those that emanate from the devil: the former are always sweet and peaceful inducing the soul to confidence and humility, while the latter are intense, restless, and violent, leading to discouragement and mistrust, or else to presumption and self-will. We must, therefore, constantly reject all that does not show signs of peace, submission, sweetness, and confidence, all of which bear, as it were, the impression of the seal of God; this point is a very important one for the whole of our life.

— Excerpt from an undated letter written to an unnamed sister.

# Notes

1. Jean-Pierre de Caussade, *Abandonment to Divine Providence* (New York: Doubleday Image, 1975).

2. Jean-Pierre de Caussade, *Abandonment to Divine Providence* (St. Louis: Herder, 1921), 2.

## BOOKS & MEDIA

The Daughters of St. Paul operate book and media centers at the following addresses. Visit, call, or write the one nearest you today, or find us at www.pauline.org.

**CALIFORNIA**

3908 Sepulveda Blvd, Culver City, CA 90230310-397-8676

935 Brewster Avenue, Redwood City, CA 94063650-369-4230

5945 Balboa Avenue, San Diego, CA 92111858-565-9181

**FLORIDA**

145 S.W. 107th Avenue, Miami, FL 33174305-559-6715

**HAWAII**

1143 Bishop Street, Honolulu, HI 96813808-521-2731

Neighbor Islands call:866-521-2731

**ILLINOIS**

172 North Michigan Avenue, Chicago, IL 60601312-346-4228

**LOUISIANA**

4403 Veterans Memorial Blvd, Metairie, LA 70006504-887-7631

**MASSACHUSETTS**

885 Providence Hwy, Dedham, MA 02026781-326-5385

**MISSOURI**

9804 Watson Road, St. Louis, MO 63126314-965-3512

**NEW YORK**

64 W. 38th Street, New York, NY 10018212-754-1110

**PENNSYLVANIA**

Philadelphia—relocating215-676-9494

**SOUTH CAROLINA**

243 King Street, Charleston, SC 29401843-577-0175

**VIRGINIA**

1025 King Street, Alexandria, VA 22314703-549-3806

**CANADA**

3022 Dufferin Street, Toronto, ON M6B 3T5416-781-9131

¡También somos su fuente para libros,
videos y música en español!

## TODAY'S QUESTIONS. TIMELESS ANSWERS.

Looking for time-tested guidance for the dilemmas of the spiritual life? Find it in the company of the wise spiritual masters of our Catholic tradition.

*Christ in Our Midst: Wisdom from Caryll Houselander*

*Comfort in Hardship: Wisdom from Thérèse of Lisieux*

*Courage in Chaos: Wisdom from Francis de Sales*

*Inner Peace: Wisdom from Jean-Pierre de Caussade*

*Intimacy in Prayer: Wisdom from Bernard of Clairvaux*

*Life's Purpose: Wisdom from John Henry Newman*

*Path of Holiness: Wisdom from Catherine of Siena*

*Peace in Prayer: Wisdom from Teresa of Avila*

*Secrets of the Spirit: Wisdom from Luis Martinez*

*A Simple Life: Wisdom from Jane Frances de Chantal*

*Solace in Suffering: Wisdom from Thomas à Kempis*

*Strength in Darkness: Wisdom from John of the Cross*